FRANCIS FRITH

WAKEFIELD AND THE FIVE TOWNS

PHOTOGRAPHIC MEMORIES

ROBERT PREEDY has spent his working life in broadcasting both with the BBC and ITV. His various jobs have included cameraman, researcher, promotions producer and latterly continuity announcer for Yorkshire Television. In radio he worked for most of the regional stations and now presents a country music show for the BBC. With a keen interest in local studies, he has published twenty books on the history of cinemas, theatres, and other popular amusements from Victorian times. He has made a detailed study of the development of fairgrounds and pleasure parks and has written two books on the history of roller coasters. Other recent books include the story of Batley Variety Club and the histories of the pop pirate stations Radio 270 and Radio Caroline North. Away from broadcasting and writing, his business interests include running a cinema in Wetherby, where he now lives.

FRANCIS FRITH'S
PHOTOGRAPHIC MEMORIES

WAKEFIELD
AND THE
FIVE TOWNS

PHOTOGRAPHIC MEMORIES

ROBERT PREEDY

First published in the United Kingdom in 2004 by
Frith Book Company Ltd

Limited Hardback Subscribers Edition Published in 2004
ISBN 1-85937-926-5

Paperback Edition 2004
ISBN 1-85937-840-4

British Library Cataloguing in Publication Data

Francis Frith's Wakefield and the Five Towns -
Photographic Memories
Robert Preedy

Frith Book Company Ltd
Frith's Barn, Teffont,
Salisbury, Wiltshire SP3 5QP
Tel: +44 (0) 1722 716 376
Email: info@francisfrith.co.uk
www.francisfrith.co.uk

Printed and bound in Great Britain

Front Cover: **WAKEFIELD,** *Wood Street c1950* w464005t
Frontispiece: **OSSETT,** *Market Place c1955* o48002

*The colour-tinting is for illustrative purposes only, and is not intended
to be historically accurate*

CONTENTS

FRANCIS FRITH
VICTORIAN PIONEER

FRANCIS FRITH, founder of the world-famous photographic archive, was a complex and multi-talented man. A devout Quaker and a highly successful Victorian businessman, he was philosophical by nature and pioneering in outlook.

By 1855 he had already established a wholesale grocery business in Liverpool, and sold it for the astonishing sum of £200,000, which is the equivalent today of over £15,000,000. Now a very rich man, he was able to indulge his passion for travel. As a child he had pored over travel books written by early explorers, and his fancy and imagination had been stirred by family holidays to the sublime mountain regions of Wales and Scotland. 'What lands of spirit-stirring and enriching scenes and places!' he had written. He was to return to these scenes of grandeur in later years to 'recapture the thousands of vivid and tender memories', but with a different purpose. Now in his thirties, and captivated by the new science of photography, Frith set out on a series of pioneering journeys up the Nile and to the Near East that occupied him from 1856 until 1860.

INTRIGUE AND EXPLORATION

These far-flung journeys were packed with intrigue and adventure. In his life story, written when he was sixty-three, Frith tells of being held captive by bandits, and of fighting 'an awful midnight battle to the very point of surrender with a deadly pack of hungry, wild dogs'. Wearing flowing Arab costume, Frith arrived at Akaba by camel sixty years before Lawrence of Arabia, where he encountered 'desert princes and rival sheikhs, blazing with jewel-hilted swords'.

He was the first photographer to venture beyond the sixth cataract of the Nile. Africa was still the mysterious 'Dark Continent', and Stanley and Livingstone's historic meeting was a decade into the future. The conditions for picture taking confound belief. He laboured for hours in his wicker dark-room in the sweltering heat of the desert, while the volatile chemicals fizzed dangerously in their trays. Back in London he exhibited his photographs and was 'rapturously cheered' by members of the Royal Society. His reputation as a photographer was made overnight.

VENTURE OF A LIFE-TIME

Characteristically, Frith quickly spotted the opportunity to create a new business as a specialist publisher of photographs. He lived in an era of immense and sometimes violent change.

For the poor in the early part of Victoria's reign work was exhausting and the hours long, and people had precious little free time to enjoy themselves. Most had no transport other than a cart or gig at their disposal, and rarely travelled far beyond the boundaries of their own town or village. However, by the 1870s the railways had threaded their way across the country, and Bank Holidays and half-day Saturdays had been made obligatory by Act of Parliament. All of a sudden the working man and his family were able to enjoy days out and see a little more of the world.

With typical business acumen, Francis Frith foresaw that these new tourists would enjoy having souvenirs to commemorate their days out. In 1860 he married Mary Ann Rosling and set out on a new career: his aim was to photograph every city, town and village in Britain. For the next thirty years he travelled the country by train and by pony and trap, producing fine photographs of seaside resorts and beauty spots that were keenly bought by millions of Victorians. These prints were painstakingly pasted into family albums and pored over during the dark nights of winter, rekindling precious memories of summer excursions.

THE RISE OF FRITH & CO

Frith's studio was soon supplying retail shops all over the country. To meet the demand he gathered about him a small team of photographers, and published the work of independent artist-photographers of the calibre of Roger Fenton and Francis Bedford. In order to gain some understanding of the scale of Frith's business one only has to look at the catalogue issued by Frith & Co in 1886: it runs to some 670 pages, listing not only many thousands of views of the British Isles but also many photographs of most European countries, and China, Japan, the USA and Canada - note the sample page shown on page 9 from the hand-written Frith & Co ledgers recording the pictures. By 1890 Frith had created the greatest specialist photographic publishing company in the world, with over 2,000 sales outlets - more than the combined number that Boots and WH Smith have today! The picture on the next page shows the Frith & Co display board at Ingleton in the Yorkshire Dales (left of window). Beautifully constructed with a mahogany frame and gilt inserts, it could display up to a dozen local scenes.

POSTCARD BONANZA

The ever-popular holiday postcard we know today took many years to develop. In 1870 the Post Office issued the first plain cards, with a pre-printed stamp on one face. In 1894 they allowed other publishers' cards to be sent through the mail with an attached adhesive halfpenny stamp. Demand grew rapidly, and in 1895 a new size of postcard was permitted called the court card, but there was little room for illustration. In 1899, a year after Frith's death, a new card measuring 5.5 x 3.5 inches became the standard format, but it was not until 1902 that the divided back came into being, so that the address and message could be on one face and a full-size illustration on the other. Frith & Co were in the vanguard of postcard development: Frith's sons Eustace and Cyril continued their father's monumental task, expanding the number of views offered to the public and recording more and more places in Britain, as the coasts and countryside were opened up to mass travel.

Francis Frith had died in 1898 at his villa in Cannes, his great project still growing. The archive he created continued in business for another seventy years. By 1970 it contained over a third of a million pictures showing 7,000 British towns and villages.

FRANCIS FRITH'S LEGACY

Frith's legacy to us today is of immense significance and value, for the magnificent archive of evocative photographs he created provides a unique record of change in the cities, towns and villages throughout Britain over a century and more. Frith and his fellow studio photographers revisited locations many times down the years to update their views, compiling for us an enthralling and colourful pageant of British life and character.

We are fortunate that Frith was dedicated to recording the minutiae of everyday life. For it is this sheer wealth of visual data, the painstaking chronicle of changes in dress, transport, street layouts, buildings, housing, engineering and landscape that captivates us so much today. His remarkable images offer us a powerful link with the past and with the lives of our ancestors.

THE VALUE OF THE ARCHIVE TODAY

Computers have now made it possible for Frith's many thousands of images to be accessed almost instantly. Frith's images are increasingly used as visual resources, by social historians, by researchers into genealogy and ancestry, by architects and town planners, and by teachers involved in local history projects.

In addition, the archive offers every one of us an opportunity to examine the places where we and our families have lived and worked down the years. Highly successful in Frith's own era, the archive is now, a century and more on, entering a new phase of popularity. Historians consider the Francis Frith Collection to be of prime national importance. It is the only archive of its kind remaining in private ownership. Francis Frith's archive is now housed in an historic timber barn in the beautiful village of Teffont in Wiltshire. Its founder would not recognize the archive office as it is today. In place of the many thousands of dusty boxes containing glass plate negatives and an all-pervading odour of photographic chemicals, there are now ranks of computer screens. He would be amazed to watch his images travelling round the world at unimaginable speeds through internet lines.

The archive's future is both bright and exciting. Francis Frith, with his unshakeable belief in making photographs available to the greatest number of people, would undoubtedly approve of what is being done today with his lifetime's work. His photographs depicting our shared past are now bringing pleasure and enlightenment to millions around the world a century and more after his death.

WAKEFIELD AND THE FIVE TOWNS
AN INTRODUCTION

IN THIS book we look back to a time when trains and trams ran like clockwork, when our pleasures were satisfied locally at the corner cinema, and when it was possible to enjoy a cycle ride on quiet country lanes. This was also a time when neighbourhood doors were left unlocked and children could play safely in streets and woods.

These evocative photographs from the Francis Frith Collection remind us of those seemingly carefree days when we could afford less, but were satisfied with what we had. The scenes show a more local and leisurely life, where the community offered self-help and surveillance and local factory owners provided employment from apprenticeship to retirement.

The development of Wakefield and the Five Towns (Normanton, Featherstone, Castleford, Knottingley and Pontefract) was shaped by a handful of landowners; their country estates retained rural values, while their urban land was for wealth creation. Centuries ago, land hereabouts was gifted as a reward for allegiance to William the Conqueror. Later, the Dissolution of the Monasteries released more valuable estates to the favoured few; and when the Industrial Revolution gathered pace, landowners were well placed to lease out mineral rights or to work the

reserves themselves.

Wakefield and the Five Towns formed a loose grouping in the 18th century - possibly against the threat of the burgeoning wealth being created by the Industrial Revolution to the north around Leeds and Bradford, and to the south at Doncaster and Sheffield. The potteries in the Five towns are also thought to have marketed themselves as a geographical composite.

All around here we have reminders of this rich past, including Nostell Priory, Pontefract Castle, Roman remains at Castleford, the proud Town Hall at Ossett, John Carr's architectural legacy in Horbury, the Grammar School in Normanton, mining memories around Featherstone and coaching days in Ferrybridge.

In Wakefield, many of the street names are reminders of its history. Along Bread Street, for instance, a bakehouse was established in 1306 - all bakers had to use this communal oven. In the Middle Ages, water ran from a muddy field near the centre of today's city: the road is now called the Springs. The Elizabethan Gallery, built in 1591 as a school, has in recent times been renovated and used for exhibitions. For 200 years up until 1963, sheep and cattle were sold on a fortnightly market just off the main shopping streets. And until 1771, an even more unpleasant odour could be found at the Softs, an open sewer that cascaded down Kirkgate and eventually reached the river.

The city's mercantile past can be admired in the rich architecture all around the centre. Here from the turn of the 19th century prominent buildings told visitors that Wakefield was a place of prosperous industry. The riverside offered the first encouragement to trade when the Aire and Calder Navigation Company opened up links with Hull and the continent nearby. Once the railway was built in 1840, a network of new industries opened up between Yorkshire and Lancashire. This new prosperity allowed the rich merchants to display their wealth by building grand new houses and developments.

Wood Street contains the municipal reflection of this affluence, with the old Mechanics' Institute, the Town Hall, the Court House and the West Riding County Hall, all built in the 19th century. St John's Square was a risky venture when it was conceived, but it remains a very attractive collection of houses arranged around the church. The Grammar School and the Girls' High School show the importance placed on education, while the austere Wakefield Prison, very close to the city centre, displays the harsher side of life.

In 1903 the famous sculptor Barbara Hepworth was born at 15 Duke of York Street, and her work is displayed in the Art Gallery and near County Hall. Five years earlier, in 1898, Henry Moore was born in Castleford. His impressive sculptures are now in galleries worldwide.

Moore's Castleford would have been a very noisy and smoky place. The town was surrounded by massive collieries and glass works; the river was central to this activity, with 'Tom Pudding' barges wending their way in non-stop procession up and down the waterway. Castleford's origins can be traced back to Roman times, when the army found this an easy point to traverse the river and continue their conquest northwards.

Pontefract also has a Roman history, but its main development was in the Middle Ages. After the Norman Conquest in 1066, a wooden castle was established here by the Norman army to control the vast territory of Yorkshire. Slowly the castle was rebuilt in stone, and once it was in Royal ownership its importance grew even more. The Crusaders of the 12th century probably introduced the liquorice plant to Pontefract, and from that grew a hugely important industry; it still flourishes today, but the liquorice roots are now grown in Turkey and Iran. Although the town was once the main centre of West Yorkshire, its importance had declined by the 18th century; but very prosperous houses can still be seen around the centre.

The wool and textile industry contributed much to the wealth of this area. Around Horbury and Ossett grew factories making shoddy and mungo. Today we would call it recycling: old clothes and fabrics were torn apart and re-processed to begin life again as new textiles.

Knottingley's industrial origins contain lime quarrying, glass blowing, potteries and shipbuilding. A new commercial centre replaced the original village of Featherstone, two miles south, after the rapid growth in coal mining. Normanton's expansion also followed mining and the arrival of the railway, and like Featherstone, led to the creation of a new town centre.

In all these towns there are so many reminders of a rich industrial past. The north-south divide may continue to drain our county of much investment and skills, but nothing can erase the past; thanks to the skill of the Frith photographers, we can look back proudly at what was once the manufacturing powerhouse of the nation.

WAKEFIELD

WAKEFIELD
The Bull Ring c1960 W464035

Looking towards the Bull Ring from Union Street, we see (right) the rebuilt Strafford Hotel and the former shops, now a café bar. At the centre is the magnificent Cloth Hall building at the head of Cross Street. The Bull Ring is now partly pedestrianised, offering a relaxed starting point for a walk to the cathedral.

WAKEFIELD
The Bull Ring c1960
W464048

For much of the 20th century the 35cwt statue of Queen Victoria graced the centre of the Bull Ring. This was unveiled on 15 February 1905 (the same day that the foundation stone was laid for the Drury Lane Library), and at that time Queen Victoria looked north. She was taken to Clarence Park on 10 July 1950, and since her return from Clarence Park in 1985, she now surveys the scene to the left towards Wood Street junction.

WAKEFIELD, *The Bull Ring c1960* W464050

The Market Place was renamed the Bull Ring in 1910, to recall the 'sport' of bull baiting a century before. In the centre of the Market Place, a busy intersection even before cars were invented, was the Toll Booth (demolished 1857) and the Boy and Barrel Inn (removed 1898). The dominant row of shops has been modernised, but the bus station (centre right), which opened on September 1952, has now been moved a hundred yards to the east.

► **WAKEFIELD**
Cross Square 1949 W464001a

At the head of Cross Street the market cross once stood, from 1707 to 1866. Cross Street is now traffic free down to the cathedral and Kirkgate. The magnificent Grand Clothing Hall, left, remains. Designed in an Italian Renaissance style by Percy Robinson (1879-1950), it opened in 1906. Robinson also designed the old Leeds Fire Station. Hartley Shaw's household furnishings emporium (right) is now an optician's, but the Black Rock next door, its name commemorating the coal industry, is still a thriving pub. The café at the end of the row is also flourishing.

▼ **WAKEFIELD**
Cross Square 1949 W464001

WAKEFIELD
Westmorland Street
c1960 W464036

This prime retail area, remaining little changed today, leads off the Bull Ring. Long gone, of course, is the variety of shops, superseded by new all-encompassing shopping centres. The Co-op Superette (right) is now a wool shop, but the Borough Market Hotel beyond still thrives. At the end of the street is a glimpse of the New Dolphin Inn (1909), once close to the wooden framed Six Chimneys house and shops. Looking left past Westmorland House is Brook Street, which leads to the Market Hall.

WAKEFIELD, *Market Place c1965* W464056

This scene is little changed in forty years. Market Place still contains Cresswell's, a seafood shop (left), and a coffee bar beyond. The Shakespeare, right, is 'as we like it' these days, a charity shop. The Market Hall, (centre), opened on 23 April 1964; it cost £289,000 and holds 87 stalls, and replaced the old one which was in use from 29 August 1851.

WAKEFIELD
Kirkgate c1955 W464013

This is now a very different scene at the start of Kirkgate. All the shops on the right were swept away for the 1960s redevelopment that saw the building of the multi-storey flats, Manor House, Trinity House and Warren House. These now tower over the shops, which incorporate a main entrance to the Ridings shopping centre (its foundation stone was laid in December 1981, and it was fully open in 1983). More familiar is the view on the left, with the old Regal Cinema (1935-1993) just discernable and beyond that the Harewood Arms. At the bottom of the road was the start of the many waterside mills and warehouses. Kirkgate station (rebuilt 1867) remains as a fine example of early railway architecture.

WAKEFIELD, *Kirkgate c1965* W464032

Woolworth's store, seen here at the end of this section of Kirkgate (centre), draws shoppers down this precinct past the shops on the right, built in the early 1960s. Cantors furniture store (right) is now a building society, while part of the Burton clothing store, centre, is now McDonalds.

16

WAKEFIELD, *Upper Kirkgate c1955* W464003

Here we are at the lower end of Kirkgate, all car-free today. Behind us is the long established Woolworth's store, and the shop buildings on the right are also long-standing, with only cosmetic changes - like the removal of the chimneys and dormers from the central building.

WAKEFIELD
Kirkgate c1965
W464055

Further up the hill, opposite the cathedral, are the large department stores of Marks & Spencer and British Home Stores. The area became a bustling precinct after the removal of the fence and bank (right) in 1976, and gives shoppers a relaxing resting point in front of the cathedral.

WAKEFIELD, *Kirkgate c1950* W464012

The cathedral, behind the fence (left), looks out onto the main retail area of the city, with Marks & Spencer's store (centre) still thriving. The George Hotel (right) and the independent traders were replaced in the 1960s by a BHS store. This area is free of traffic and is a little oasis in the bustling centre of Wakefield.

WAKEFIELD, *The Cathedral c1950* W464008

There has been a church on this site for a thousand years. After many alterations and additions, the parish church of
All Saints attained cathedral status in 1888. The oldest part now dates from 1329, while its spire, at 247 feet, is the highest in
Yorkshire.

► **WAKEFIELD**
Kirkgate c1965
W464040

Kirkgate (its name comes from the Danish words for 'church way') is seen here from the west end of the cathedral. This shopping complex with its sweeping lines still contains large national shops, and seems unthreatened by the new Ridings Centre, off to the left down Southgate. Until 1938 the City Time Ball over a jeweller's store was linked to Greenwich, and dropped down its tube at 10am and 1pm. This upper part of Kirkgate was declared traffic free in 1976.

◄ **WAKEFIELD**
The Chantry c1950
W464002

Here we see two extremes of worship - the cathedral in the distance, and the more modest St Mary-on-the-Bridge. Over to the right once stood the massive King's Mill, used for grinding corn from 1872 until 1933, when it was demolished to make way for the parallel new road bridge. The final cargo of corn arrived by barge from Hull in September 1931.

▲ **WAKEFIELD,** *The Old Bridge and the Chantry c1955* W464021e

The bridge over the River Calder is no longer the main arterial road from the south, having been superseded by the new bridge of 1933. This now protects St Mary's Chantry from worse pollution, and gives this haven a slightly more contemplative feel. The Chantry, now one of only four in the country, was built to offer comfort to travellers entering Wakefield from the south. It was licensed in 1356 and continued for worship until the Dissolution in 1548; by 1638 it was in a state of decay. A dealer in old clothes subsequently used it. The frontage was replaced in 1848, but being built of Caen stone, it succumbed to erosion and was later remodelled in local material. Its original front was re-erected in Kettlethorpe Hall, where it remains, in good order, at the end of the lake.

◄ **WAKEFIELD**
The Grammar School c1955 W464022

This was originally the West Riding Proprietary School, built at a cost of £15,000 and opened by its President, Earl Fitzwilliam on 6 August 1834. It offered a more varied education than the formal syllabus of the Grammar School, founded in 1591 and based at the Elizabethan Hall near to the outdoor market. This area eventually became very crowded, and surrounded by slaughterhouses and dank infested alleys. When the Proprietary School fell into financial difficulties twenty years after opening, the Grammar School purchased it at auction in December 1854. Since then many additions have been added to give us the present day Grammar School, which celebrated four hundred years with a visit from the Queen in March 1992.

► **WAKEFIELD**
Clarence Park c1960 W464046

This was the first of the open spaces provided for the workers of Wakefield at the end of the 19th century. The Duke of Clarence opened the Technical and Art College on the site of the old Thornes House in 1891, and this adjacent park (29 acres), once grazing land, was opened to the public on 6 July 1893, the day of the marriage of the Duke of York. The bandstand, left, opens out into a huge amphitheatre for musical concerts; built in 1926, it replaced the original less convenient stand at the top of Lowe Hill. The Queen Victoria statue was moved from the Bull Ring to Clarence Park in 1950 and remained here until November 1984, when it was cleaned and returned to its original site.

◀ WAKEFIELD
Holmefield House
c1950 W464007

Adjoining Clarence Park is the slightly smaller (14-acre) park surrounding Holmefield House. This private estate was developed in 1833 by the Wakefield solicitor and Clerk of Barnsley Canal Company Thomas Foljambe (1775-1851), part of a larger scheme to build a number of grand houses. Only Holmefield House was built (it was much altered by Major Barker from 1864), although Foljambe built a large house on Thornes Lane from stone discarded during the construction of the Manchester & Leeds Railway at Horbury. His workers at Thorne Mills erected a drinking fountain to Major Barker's memory in Clarence Park in 1893.

23

WAKEFIELD
Holmefield House c1960
W464049

The house and land was bought by the corporation for £5,500 and opened to the public during the Peace Celebrations in July 1919. The ground floor of Holmefield House was used as a café, and the upper portion as the first City Museum (from 1923 to 1956). On the estate was a Doric pillar from Wakefield's Market Cross, dismantled in 1866 - other pillars went to Clarke Hall and Alverthorpe Hall. A pinnacle from the cathedral also graced the grounds of Holmefield House. Today the gardens in front of the house form part of the beer garden for the Holmfield Arms.

WAKEFIELD, *Holmefield House c1960* W464047

The extended garden of the house is now a forecourt for a modern hotel built on the site of the old rock garden, which used to be the kitchen garden with glasshouses. Next to the flagpole we can just see what appears to be the old cathedral pinnacle.

WAKEFIELD
The Lake, Thornes Park
c1950 W464009

Thornes Park was the third of the parks to come under public ownership. About 87 acres are dedicated to recreation, including this charming waterfowl lake used for ice-skating in cold winters. In the centre of the estate on higher ground is the site of the old Thornes House, completed in 1781 to the designs of John Carr for the clothing merchant James Milnes. The house was a scaled-down version of Harewood House near Leeds, also created by Carr.

WAKEFIELD, *Thornes Park c1960* W464006

Here we see the gardener's house; it was originally surrounded by a kitchen garden and glasshouses to provide fresh produce all year long for the magnificent red brick Thornes House with its impressive 200-foot façade. The bricks came from Milnes's works, and timber was imported from Russia, where his cloth exports flourished. Milnes rivalled the Denisons of Leeds as the county's biggest cloth exporter, and in 1778 he married the heiress of another prosperous Leeds textile merchant, Hans Buck. The marriage dowry amounted to £100,000 – the money was quickly spent on Thornes House.

▶ **WAKEFIELD**

The Rose Gardens, Thornes Park c1955 W464004

Next to the gardener's house is the present-day rose garden, with delightful walkways and tropical houses. The last occupant of Thornes House was the Morley MP, Charles Milnes Gaskell. After this the house was used as a military hospital during the First World War, and was sold to the Council in 1919 for £18,500. It opened as a public park in August 1924, completing the 153 acres of breathing space we now enjoy. The house was used as a school from 1921, but it burned down on 15 July 1951. Wakefield College now stands on the site.

◄ **WAKEFIELD**
Nostell Priory c1955
W464025

Set in magnificent pleasure grounds and gardens, Nostell was built on the site of a 12th-century priory dedicated to St Oswald. After the Dissolution it was converted into a dwelling, and in 1650 was acquired by the Winn family, who have lived here ever since. This new house, built to the north of the old priory, was built in 1735. The parkland was first enclosed as a deer park in 1604, and has subsequently provided peace and tranquillity for National Trust visitors since 1953.

OSSETT: TEXTILES, CLOTHING, SHODDY AND MUNGO

OSSETT
Market Place c1955 O48002

Reflecting the prosperity of Ossett at the turn of the 20th century, the Town Hall still stands proudly at the end of the Market Place. Built on the site of the former Grammar School, the Town Hall opened in June 1908 at a cost of £23,000. Beneath the clock tower is the town's motto: 'Inutile Utile ex Arte'. This means 'useless things are made useful by skill', which accurately describes the industry that allowed the town to flourish: its woollen mills later specialised in recycling old rags to feed the local works. In 1912 Ossett had 90 rag merchants and 18 mungo and shoddy factories. Around the Market Place are many important commercial concerns like the old London City and Midland Bank of 1892 (left), now minus its cupola. This area is now pedestrianised, and contains the 1928 war memorial, which was moved here from Kingsway in 2001. The old Pickard Memorial Fountain (1893), later removed to Green Park, was a turning point for motorbuses after the disappearance of the trams that terminated here from 1908 to 1933. Also remembered with affection is the magnificent Palladium cinema, which entertained the town from 1913 to 1961.

◄**OSSETT**
The Green
c1955 O48004

This view is now much changed. The Green Congregational Chapel replaced an earlier one (1850-1882), and opened in 1883 at a cost of £5690. It was replaced by a more easily maintained place of worship after 1973.

◄ **OSSETT**
Station Road
c1955 O48003

Station Road was laid out in the late 19th century, and contained many prominent institutions. Here we see the Yorkshire Penny Bank (left) in the 1893 building which was originally the post office. To the right is the Liberal Club, also of 1893, and further along is the old Mechanics' Institute (1889) with its own collection of over 800 books. Today the building houses the town's comprehensive public library. Ossett's GNR railway station was open until 1964.

◄ **OSSETT**
Wesley Street c1955 O48001

The classical façade of the Wesley Methodist Chapel (1868-1962) dominated this part of the street running off Market Place. Also along Wesley Street were a number of impressive houses built during the 19th century for wealthy mill owners. Wesley House, set back on the left, was home to William Garside, a prosperous dyer. The house and land was bought in 1889 by Edward Clay (1844-1921), who was the town's first mayor in 1890. Here he lived and expanded his rag processing works, which were originally established in 1870. The tradition continues: the family firm is still here, manufacturing textile products reclaimed from charity shops' unwanted clothing.

HORBURY: AN ARCHITECT'S LEGACY

HORBURY
High Street c1955 H214002

The heart of the town has all the popular shops together and easily accessible to 1950s shoppers. Behind the imposing Co-op building on the left was the old cinema, which became a ballroom once the new Co-op Cinema opened in 1930. This ran in School Lane until 1967.

HORBURY
Westfield Road
c1955 H214006

This imposing building at the junction of Westfield Road and Wakefield Road originated as the United Counties Bank in 1910, later becoming Barclay's. Now, like so many similar edifices, it prospers as a public house. Trams from Wakefield through Horbury on to Ossett ran past here from 15 August 1904 to 24 July 1932.

HORBURY, *Westfield Road and the Town Hall c1955* H214010

Now slightly nearer the town centre, we see more commercial and municipal buildings. The bus offices on the left stand opposite the old Midland Bank and the Town Hall and Library.

HORBURY
Queen Street c1955
H214009

Off the High Street is
Queen Street, taking us up
towards St Peter's Church.
On the left we see the long-
established Andrassy's
butcher's shop – it opened
in 1886. Bradley's butcher's
shop next to the stop sign
(right) is still trading. The
town's first gas lamp was
also on Queen Street.
Horbury's wealth was
created from the woollen
trade from the 13th century,
and the Savile family were
dominant traders in later
years. In 1700 the Duke of
Leeds held the manorial
rights, and these passed to
Mr Lane Fox on his marriage
to the Duke's daughter.

▼ **HORBURY,** *The Town Hall and the Library, Westfield c1955* H214018

Andrew Carnegie, the Scottish entrepreneur who made his fortune in Pittsburgh steel, was also a devoted philanthropist. He endowed many public libraries at the turn of the 20th century. Here, right, is Horbury's Carnegie Free Library, built in 1905 and opened on 14 February 1906. The Town Hall next door is built on the site of a house and garden. Further to the right was a public convenience for gentlemen only, as were many others in the town.

▶ **HORBURY**
St Peter's Church c1955
H214005

The spire of St Peter's Church can be seen from all parts of Horbury. It was a substantial gift to the town from John Carr (1723-1807), the famous architect who never forgot his roots, even though he twice became the Lord Mayor of York. The sandstone church replaced the old Norman church of St Leonard, which was demolished in 1790; the first service at St Peter's took place on 18 May 1794. Monuments to Carr and his father hang on the wall of the church, and John Carr is interred in the vault below the vestry.

Here we look towards Cluntergate; on the right is the birthplace of John Carr. His father, Robert, was a stonemason and quarry owner, where John developed his skill with the local sandstone. It is believed that this picture was taken in August 1952; the couple are John and Dorothy Sherwood with their baby daughter Anne.

▶ **HORBURY**
County Secondary School c1955
H214016

Northfield Lane continues past John Carr's cottage, and just around the corner is this school established in 1913. In 1951 it was designated a Secondary Modern School, and it later became a Junior and Infant School in 1962. Horbury's Grammar School was in Highfield Road, where older pupils were provided with a smoking room.

HORBURY
Cluntergate c1955
H214017

If we walk along Cluntergate towards the town centre past John Carr's birthplace in the tidy cottage built by his father in 1739, we see the Cricketers Arms pub (1898) on the left. Some of the stone buildings (right) remain, but the tranquillity of fifty years ago has long been lost.

NORMANTON AND ALTOFTS: COLLIERIES AND A STAGING POST

ALTOFTS, *The Horse and Jockey 1959* A122005

Beverley's beers were certainly best at the Horse and Jockey (left) back in 1959. Now the village's oldest pub is almost the only remaining building in this picture. Gone even is W H Hattersley's general store in the circular shop (centre) - the whole area has been transformed by new housing development. Back in 1880 an orchard, stables, piggeries, a bowling green and two cottages surrounded the pub. Also in that period massive pits surrounded Altofts, and the Church of St Mary Magdalene (1890) has a window memorial to the 32 men and boys (and 53 horses) killed in the explosion at the West Riding Colliery on 2 October 1886.

NORMANTON
Market Place c1955 N159021

From the bottom of the High Street we look across Market Place to Lower Station Road - the main thoroughfare to Normanton Station. The station platform was a quarter of a mile long and could handle six trains at any one time. In the 1880s it became a staging post for immigrants on their long journey from Scandinavia to Liverpool and then to America. Over 700,000 passengers passed through Normanton each year, and the station employed 700 staff. Once other lines offered a

quicker service, Normanton declined; but it still retained maintenance services for locomotives like the Flying Scotsman. In this picture there has been little change in forty years. The Rotary Club Coronation Clock was placed here in 1953, and before that the 12ft-high John Barr fountain and horse trough was here from 1896 to 1938.

NORMANTON, *Market Place c1955* N159011

The Central Market (centre left) opened in 1901, but was replaced recently by a more modern facility opposite. Happily the façade of the old market has been kept, and is now a walkway to the High Street. Young's drapery shop next to it is now a bank.

▶ NORMANTON
High Street c1955
N159009

This is the main shopping area of the town; the architecture matches the period of rapid development after the railway arrived. The Assembly Rooms, dominating the right side of the street, opened in 1888 and was used for dances, lectures and public entertainment. From 1910 it was converted to the Palace, the first of four cinemas in the town. At the top of the High Street next to the Majestic Cinema (1931-1959) are the old swimming baths, opened in 1926, and mostly financed by the miner's union.

◀ NORMANTON
The Library c1955
N159007

Local pit manager Sir William Garforth, who donated 250 books, opened this Carnegie Library on 29 May 1907. The library was in the grounds of Hawhill Park - a perfect place for learning and recreation. Books were issued here for the final time on Friday 26 October 2001. Since then, a more modern facility has been opened next to the new swimming baths.

▲ **NORMANTON,** *The Grammar School c1955* N159003

The small section with the bell tower is the only remaining part of the old Freeston High School; it was built in 1592 with an endowment from John Freeston, who lived at Altofts Hall. In 1867 the Church School was built opposite, and the Grammar School began to struggle - fee-paying students were sent to the cheaper option. The Grammar School was then rebuilt on its three-acre site and opened on 25 October 1897 by the Earl of Crewe. Most of the structure in the picture has gone, but the present Normanton Junior School is still looked over by the old bell tower.

◄ **NORMANTON**
*The Girls'
Grammar
School c1955*
N159014

Next to the Grammar School was the Girls' School, which opened in May 1912 to educate 150 pupils. This fine building was demolished in the late 1990s when houses were built on the site.

◄**NORMANTON**
Hawhill Park c1955
N159015

This ten-acre park was purchased by the council with the help of donations in 1904 from the landowner, Mrs Maynell Ingram of Temple Newsam House, Leeds. When she died later in the year, more land was also bought. Part of it was used as a rubbish tip, but landscaping began in 1905 with the laying out of the first bowling green. Swings and slides and a roundabout were installed for youngsters at a cost of £59. The cenotaph war memorial, left, and the boating pond are still here for the residents of the town.

◄ NORMANTON
Church Walk
c1965 N159025

A short walk from the old Grammar School is the parish church of All Saints. Here in the graveyard can be found reminders of local landowners like the Frobishers, the Freestons and the Newlands. There is also a poignant reminder of danger in the everyday lives of working people on the gravestone of Caleb Russell, who was killed on the Midland Railway in 1889 aged 22.

◄ NORMANTON
Hawhill Park c1955
N159018

This rose garden was the site of Hawhill Park's first bowling green. Behind the roses are the ornamental gates and the spring and summer gardens opened in April 1959 by Ernest Jones, president of the National Union of Mine Workers, to commemorate a centenary of the Yorkshire Branch.

► **NORMANTON**
Hawhill Park c1955
N159019

Just near the boating lake is the old bandstand, now with only its base - the upper structure fell into disrepair and was removed. Hawhill Park is still a well-maintained recreation facility for the town; it reflects well on the foresight of the town's elders, who purchased the land in spite of much opposition from town centre traders at the turn of the 20th century.

◄ NORMANTON
Hawhill Park,
the Bowling Green
c1960 N159027

Here behind the Bowling Green is the old Primitive Methodist Church (centre), which opened in 1902. To the right is the site of the Isolation and Smallpox Hospital, where groceries and provisions were left outside for later collection by the matron. Instead of being demolished, the hospital was set alight by the fire brigade to kill any remaining germs.

CASTLEFORD: SCULPTURES, GLASS AND OUR DAILY BREAD

CASTLEFORD, *The River Aire c1955* C257017a

Two mighty rivers, the Aire and the Calder, join at Castleford, and water power began the industrial revolution in this old Roman settlement. Here the Aire used to drive the grinding wheels of the Queen's Mill (centre); it was taken over in 1921 by the Natural Food Company, led by the health innovator Dr Thomas Allinson, who firmly believed that bread was better for you 'wi' nowt taken out'. The company still occupies the mill, but the water wheel that provided so much power turned for the final time in 1973. The Aire and Calder Navigation Company was formed near here in 1698, and canals opened in 1775 and 1826.

CASTLEFORD
Carlton Street
c1965 C257028

We are looking down the main shopping area to the old Market Hall, which was partly demolished in 1992. The shell remains as a walkway through to Carlton Street, and it stands next to the 1905 Carnegie Library. This scene has changed little in forty years, apart from being pedestrianised in 1994.

CASTLEFORD, *Carlton Street c1955* C257017b

The clock above the Market Hall (centre) was a favourite rendezvous point for many courting couples on their way to the theatre and cinemas. On the left many of the shops remain, while opposite the library is one of the main entrances to the new Carlton Lanes shopping centre. The sculptor Henry Moore, the son of a miner, was born in 1898 at 30 Roundhill Road. Bricks from the house, demolished in 1974, now form a wall around a commemorative garden.

◄**CASTLEFORD**
Redhill c1955
C257011

On the road to Airedale, Redhill, named after the colour of the soil, used to be a narrow winding road; but with the development of the Parkhill estate in 1947, a cutting was made through here to provide quicker access.

◀ CASTLEFORD
The Bus Station
c1965 C257027

When the bus station opened on 20 May 1963, much Castleford history was lost with the demolition of the Queen's Head Hotel and Wainwright Street. Gone also was the site of two former glass works, now just a memory. Just a memory, too, is the nearby old Theatre Royal, which offered a variety of entertainment from 1873 to 1955. The town's coat of arms with the motto 'Audaciter et Sincere' ('boldly and frankly') perhaps sum up the municipal desire to be modern and up-to-date.

◀ CASTLEFORD
Queen's Park c1965
C257024

Overlooking Ferrybridge Road, Victoria Park was opened in time for the Queen's Diamond Jubilee in 1897. Two local landowners, the Earl of Crewe (of Fryston Hall) and John Davison Bland (of Kippax Park) donated the area, which was laid out to offer recreation and splendid views over the township.

► **CASTLEFORD**
Queen's Park c1955
C257008

Of Queen's Park's 43 acres, thirteen came from the two landowners, and a further parcel was purchased from the Earl of Crewe in 1904 to provided a park keepers' cottage, a bandstand and a pavilion. By 1909 a splendid bowling green was a new attraction, and in 1949 new greenhouses were constructed.

◄ CASTLEFORD
Valley Gardens c1965
C257019

This welcome breathing
space was laid out on a
derelict site by the railway
embankment in 1933.
Complete with a stream and
ornamental flowerbeds, the
Valley Gardens still give
much pleasure to shoppers
seeking relaxation after
shopping in nearby
Carlton Street.

CASTLEFORD
Ledsham Village c1965
C257015

Only a few miles away from the industry of Castleford, Ledsham village has remained an oasis of tranquillity. The working farm on the left gives the visitor a welcome view of unchanging rural life. The 8th-century All Saints' Church was renovated in 1871.

KIPPAX: TURNING GREEN COUNTRY ESTATES INTO BLACK GOLD

KIPPAX
The Leeds Road c1960 K72028

The church of St Mary (just visible on the horizon, centre) looks down on either side of the escarpment. On this side the semi-rural landscape has been transformed by the building of the Moorgate housing estate. Over to the south was the magnificent Kippax Park, once a hunting ground in pre-Norman days. The estate was purchased for £315 by the Bland family in 1595. A good marriage in 1663 added vast estates in Lancashire, and from this Kippax Park was built up into one of the wealthiest properties in the north. An unfortunate gambling streak in a later generation left the estate to a cousin who took the Bland name, and the family lived here until 1929 when the whole estate was sold.

Kippax was a small estate village servicing Kippax Hall and Kippax Park for three centuries before developing rapidly in the mid 19th century with the discovery of coal reserves. Kippax Colliery near Owl Wood flourished between 1858 and 1904, but it was the nearby pits of Allerton Bywater (1875-1992) and Ledston Luck (1909-1987) that transformed the village into the town it is today. To transport the huge coal output, the North Eastern Railway ran the line to nearby Castleford from 1878. Eventually, from November 1953 open cast mining encroached even on the land surrounding Kippax Park, and by 1959 the 300ft-long house was totally demolished, leaving the farmland we see today. Once the mining finished in June 1962, over one million tons of coal had been scoured from the park to a depth of 200 feet. A gatehouse on the Castleford road is the only reminder of the Elizabethan splendour of Kippax's past.

KIPPAX
The Parish Church of St Mary the Virgin c1965 K72059

This Norman church with its distinctive herringbone masonry was restored during the 1870s. Inside are monuments to the two landowning families in the village, the Blands of Kippax Park with its 250 acres and magnificent house, and the Medhursts of Kippax Hall, once home to fervent Methodism.

KIPPAX, *High Street c1960* K72038

This is the shopping centre of Kippax, much changed on the left, but untouched on the right. A large Co-op store has replaced their smaller shop, left, but the parade of shops (centre) still thrives. The Kippax Cinema closed in 1964, depriving local children of their lively Saturday morning matinee fun. Bingo then took over for the next thirty-five years.

PONTEFRACT: LIQUORICE AND ALLSORTS

PONTEFRACT
The Castle Keep 1964 P155035

During the Middle Ages, Pontefract was at the centre of political life in West Yorkshire. In the 10th century, Pontefract lay in the royal estate of Tanshelf. The town was given its first charter in 1194, and grew rapidly in the shadow of the huge castle, where civil war was played out on a regular basis. Charles, Duke of Orleans, was captured at Agincourt and held for 13 years at the castle. Just beneath the walls of the castle is the last liquorice plant from the nursery, replanted here in 1999.

▼ **PONTEFRACT,** *The Castle Kitchens 1964* P155036

Walls six feet thick protected the castle kitchens, built after 1413 to replace less grand facilities. Here meals were prepared from fresh produce grown in the castle nursery and gardens, to feed not only the soldiers and staff but also the 240 prisoners held in the gunpowder magazine store during the 17th century.

► **PONTEFRACT**
Market Place c1965
P155039

Development along the market place grew in medieval times when wealthy merchants invested in some very grand houses. Here we see the façade of the Market Hall (left), and in the distance the Town Hall (1785) and Assembly Rooms (1882). The newsagents W H Smith (right) later moved to the old premises of the house furnishers, England's.

◄ PONTEFRACT
Market Place c1965
P155034

We are looking from the Town Hall down the grand vista of the largely 18th-century Market Place; it was known as the Shambles in the previous century, and designated for the sale of fresh meat in the 14th century. Now it is all pedestrianised, allowing shoppers a chance to relax and once again enjoy their surroundings. Barclays Bank (left) was the Bank of Leatham and Tew before 1906, and from 1776 to 1801 the Black Bull Inn occupied this 18th-century private house. The Red Lion (right) is one of the oldest inns in the town, and has a 1776 façade designed by Robert Adam for Sir Rowland Winn of Nostell Priory. Next to the Red Lion is the Market Hall, opened by Viscount Palmerston in 1860.

► PONTEFRACT
Ropergate c1965 P155017

Looking down Ropergate towards the Market Place, on the left we see the old Crescent Cinema (1926-1993), one of five picture palaces once in the town. Ropergate also had the County Court Office, right, and nearer town, the old post office. Also on the street is the office of the Pontefract Park Race Company, formed in 1919 to manage the old course established in the early 18th century. A grandstand was built in 1802 to the designs of Bernard Hartley, also the architect of the Pontefract Town Hall. In 1983 Pontefract became the longest flat racecourse in Europe.

▶ **PONTEFRACT**
St Giles' Church c1960 P155024

In front of St Giles' Church is the Buttercross (1734), used over the centuries for the sale of local dairy produce; it replaced the cross of St Oswald. Some of the 18th-century benches still survive inside the building. The parish church, behind, was founded in the 12th century, and became the parish church in 1789, incorporating a number of medieval remains.

▼ **PONTEFRACT**
Beastfair c1960 P155023

The prosperous Georgian feel of the town originates with the presence of the castle and with its role as a market town and agricultural centre. Here in Beastfair, the trade in cattle would have been brisk. The Merchants' Counting House, down Swale's Yard (right), was the meeting place for countless entrepreneurs from 1400 onwards; recently the building has been restored to an atmospheric pub. Other Pontefract trades included stone quarrying, woollen industries, rope making and mining. The Prince of Wales pit at Tanshelf opened in 1870, and by 1931 employed 19,000.

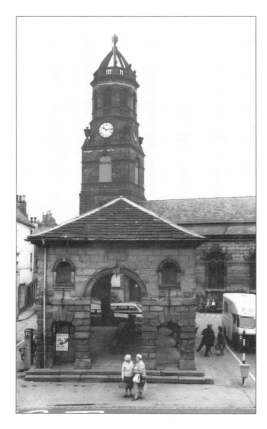

▶ **PONTEFRACT**
Town End c1965 P155018

The Crescent Cinema, far right, overlooks the now frenetic Town End roundabout. Forty years ago it was possible to relax over a pint at the Robin Hood and the New Inn (centre and right). Since this picture, both the war memorial and the New Inn have gone.

◄ **PONTEFRACT**
All Saints' Church
c1965 P155038

An Anglo-Saxon church was built across the road towards the castle, and burials are recorded here from AD700. All Saints' was gradually established between the 13th and 15th century, but was laid in ruins during the Civil War - the Royalists used the tower as lookout over the fields. The tower and transept were restored in 1831, and a new nave was built in 1967 inside the ruins (left). The church is also famous for its double helix staircase.

PONTEFRACT
Friar Valley Gardens
c1960 P155028

Pontefract General
Infirmary now overlooks the
bowling green in this oasis
of greenery near to the town
centre. Before becoming a
municipal park, these
grounds were a nursery and
market garden, whose
business included the
growing of liquorice plants.

FERRYBRIDGE AND KNOTTINGLEY: POST, POWER AND OLD ROPE

FERRYBRIDGE, *High Street c1965* F166032

Here on the High Street was the busiest part of town, once the coaching and postal services began in 1660. Half way between London and Edinburgh on the busy Great North Road, Ferrybridge was a hub, with smaller roads branching off into West Yorkshire. Fifty coaches would pass here each day, and horses were stabled in the numerous inns, many of which still survive. Post-chaises ferried travellers between the coaches and their overnight stay – this was truly a bustling place. The 1950s blocks of flats, left, replaced many small businesses, and even the Three Horseshoes Inn (centre distance) has been demolished to create a car park. In spite of once being a major postal sorting centre, the town's post office, right, closed on 27 March 2004.

FERRYBRIDGE
Front Street c1955
F166009

Looking down High Street in the opposite direction, was see the lost Three Horseshoes Inn (right) and the small cottages and shops which were replaced by the early 1960s flats. Burland's corner shop on Station Road (left) is now a food takeaway

FERRYBRIDGE, *The Village c1955* F166003

This view, opposite the Golden Lion, would be unrecognisable today. Fred Atter's grocery shop and café and the old post office went to make way for the footings of the A1 flyover, which now dominates this scene. One piece of history remains - the old Toll Bridge House in the centre distance.

FERRYBRIDGE
The Village c1955
F166004

This view of the road to nearby Knottingley has changed completely. Modern industrial units have replaced all the cottages. Mrs Wilson's local shop, left, with the delivery van outside, was also a casualty of so-called progress.

FERRYBRIDGE, *The Brotherton Fox Hotel c1955* F166015

The Great North Road swept to the right of the old Fox Inn and brought in much hotel and refreshment trade, but once the coaching days were destroyed by the railways, the inn also went into decline. Rebuilt in the 1920s, the Brotherton Fox Inn still offers a warm welcome to travellers, although the A1 is now in a cutting under the Brotherton road to the left.

FERRYBRIDGE
The Power Station c1955
F166020

Ferrybridge is ideally placed for a major power station - coal could be delivered on the adjacent River Aire, and so from 1927 for thirty years Ferrybridge 'A' Power Station, seen here, generated power for nearby towns. As demand grew, a new facility, known as Ferrybridge 'B', was opened in 1959 and offered a capacity of 282 megawatts. Ferrybridge 'C' (opened in 1968) today provides a massive output of 2,000 MW. Offices and workshops now occupy the original 1920s generator hall. Eight massive cooling towers dominate the site today, and look out over the old graveyard of St Andrew's Church.

FERRYBRIDGE
St Andrew's Church c1955 F166034

This simple, charming church was once on the flood plain of the river. It was built near the site of Fryston Hall, off Kirkhaw Lane, and when the river was in flood, marriage and other ceremonies would be held at the Mission Hall on Pontefract Road. In 1952 a decision was made to relocate the church near to the Mission Hall, and it was taken down stone by stone and rebuilt on this safer ground. The old churchyard, where Lord Haughton is buried, still remains at the original rural location in the shadows of the power station cooling towers.

▼ **FERRYBRIDGE,** *The Bridge c1955* F166001

The old bridge over the River Aire was rebuilt in 1765 and survived 32 years before its demolition in 1797. This new three-arch bridge was completed in 1804 at a cost of £24,864; on the central parapet are the names of the then 74-year-old architect John Carr and the builder, Bernard Hartley of Pontefract. The massive A1 viaduct, which opened in 1967, effectively split Ferrybridge in two, and today dwarfs the elegant bridge and its toll house. The bicentenary of this listed monument was celebrated at the Golden Lion on 6 June 2004, when beer was sold for one old penny per pint.

► **FERRYBRIDGE**
The Canal c1955
F166002

The curve of the river forces bargemen to make a skilful manoeuvre into the lock, which allows boats to travel past the weir. On many occasions when the river has been high, the jetty has felt the heavy thud of a barge - the vibration is felt just as strongly in the Golden Lion Inn.

◀ **FERRYBRIDGE**
The Canal c1955
F166012

Once this lock on the Aire and Calder Navigation opened at 10am on 20 July 1826, trade boomed between the North Sea port of Hull and the West Yorkshire industrial heartland. Grain and produce came up river from East Yorkshire, while coal, glass products, and minerals were sent from here both to London and the continent. Once the railways arrived, trade on the river declined; today the centre lock has been removed, and the lock keeper's cottage is forlorn and empty.

KNOTTINGLEY, *The Cross Roads c1955* k82020a

A much-changed junction as the old Great North Road heads north in between Pontefract and Knottingley. The road today remains very busy, even though the new A1 carries a colossal amount of traffic just to the west.

▶ **KNOTTINGLEY**
The Town c1955
K82020b

This is the middle section of the town next to the Knottingley and Goole Canal (opened 1826). On the road many of the houses remain, but the centre white one has been replaced by Saint Michael's RC Church. So many trees have grown on the land that this view is now unseen. On the mound, centre, British Waterways has constructed an amphitheatre available for community drama groups.

◀ **KNOTTINGLEY**
Hill Top c1955
K82020c

Because of industrial development, the town is built on slightly different levels. Here at the top of the western part, around the old Manor House, are some surviving cottages that used to be shops - in fact part of the white cottage was in use as the town's Post Office until March 2004.

▲ **KNOTTINGLEY,** *The Modern School c1955* K82020d

The older part of town is surrounded on all sides by water - the River Aire and two canals. Rope making was a flourishing industry both for the marine and agricultural markets. Down to the left of the Town Hall is Rope Walk, and here was the Modern School, an imposing building erected in 1842 and including as its pupils, children from barge families. In the late 1960s the Secondary Modern school transferred to new premises, and it was used as a Church School for nearly two decades until demolition twenty years ago.

◀ **KNOTTINGLEY**
Town Hall c1955 K82020e

At the end of Hill Top, before the road again crosses the canal, is the Town Hall. Financed locally by business leaders, it was opened in September 1865 by Sidney Woolf. His father was a London businessman who in 1850 had leased the Ferrybridge Pottery. Sidney, his son, was later Pontefract's Liberal MP from 1880 to 1885. The Town Hall and Mechanics' Institute offered a focus for the community and included public baths in the basement. The building costs spiralled from £1,000 to £2,400 and the owners had to take a mortgage to deal with the deficit. The financial position never improved and the building was sold at auction in 1901 to J G Lyon who gifted it to the council. Curiously a clock wasn't added to the tower until 1994.

KNOTTINGLEY, *Middle Lane High School c1967* K82030

On Spawd Bone Lane by the railway line is the new High School that opened in 1967. Years ago pupils leaving Knottingley schools would have had a choice of many trades. The town expanded rapidly from 1700 with the opening of the Aire and Calder Navigation. Even before then, shipbuilding and quarrying had flourished in this furthest inland port - some 70 miles from the sea. A dam built for King's Mills curtailed passage further west, but with the new canal system into Leeds and Wakefield, much new trade came through Knottingley. The potteries expanded, the roperies supplied the ship building trade, and once coalmines were established the limekilns were in full operation. This in turn increased river and canal journeys for these and other trades like glass making, brewing, tar works and a malting mill.

KNOTTINGLEY, *Middle Lane High School c1955*   K82023

KNOTTINGLEY
The Fire Station c1969
K82034

This modern Fire Station replaced an earlier one near to the King's Mills. Once the new Warwick housing estate was built in the late 1960s, the centre of the town moved to the west and this new Fire Station opened in March 1969. By this time the original centre of the town, around Aire Street, was an empty place following the slow closure of dozens of small shops and facilities. The Palace Cinema (1913 - 1960) at the heart of Aire Street quickly lost its audience once the town centre moved west.

KNOTTINGLEY, *The Power Station c1968* K82038

The new A1 bisected the town of Ferrybridge after 1967. The canal was still busy, with a barge taking coal loaded into a series of 'Tom Puddings' - short containers that can be coupled together in any length. They were patented in 1826 and first used on this waterway from 1865. A walk along the path in between the canal and river offers a splendid history lesson on the industrial origins of Ferrybridge and Knottingley.

KNOTTINGLEY
St Botolph's Church
c1960 K82042

A church has existed near this site since AD1110 and from 1637, after the dissolution of Meaux Abbey, the Ingram family of Temple Newsam, near Leeds, bought the land. They then endowed land and finance to the incumbent and the church flourished as the town expanded in the next century. Much rebuilding took place in 1750 and the tower was added in 1873. The East Window recalls the life of John Carter of Lime Grove, a brewer and churchwarden, who died in 1873.

KNOTTINGLEY, *St Botolph's Church and Power Station c1968* K82043

Here is a fascinating picture taken from the newly built block of flats, Low Cross Court. In the distance the modern cooling towers of Ferrybridge Power Station and in the middle distance the Aire and Calder Navigation parallel with the River Aire. The ancient church once marked the western edge of the old town and further to the left was the site of the Old Hall and Lime Grove - once homes of important landowners.

FEATHERSTONE: A NEW TOWN MADE FROM COAL

FEATHERSTONE
North Featherstone
c1955 F87027c

This was the original Featherstone up to 150 years ago, and still has the town's parish church. A mile and a half north of the present town, this was largely a farming community until the mines brought an influx of miners to the west of Purston Jaglin. The opening of major new pits - Featherstone Main (1868 - 1935) and Ackton Hall, also known as Featherstone Manor and Masham's, (1877- 1985), created a boom time for the township. That then became known as Featherstone, and this quiet village to the north became the residence of colliery owners and officials. The house pictured, Newlands on Cutsyke Road, was a smallholding; it stood opposite the largest farm in the area, which later sold ale from its back door. Later the farmhouse was converted into a full-time pub, the Bradley Arms, named after the local landowner, George Bradley, who originally sold the mineral rights for mining in 1866.

FEATHERSTONE
Purston Church and the War Memorial c1955 F87012

The church of St Thomas (built in 1878) was an important focal point in the township of Purston Jaglin that developed rapidly after the sinking of coalmines. The Church School had opened in 1820 and was extended in 1874. The Lancashire & Yorkshire Railway opened a station in 1848 for coal transport, and over the next hundred years Featherstone was a lively town, only marred by the spectre of the massacres in 1905: after a pay cut, two protesting miners were killed and many more injured by the militia.

FEATHERSTONE, *The Town Hall c1955* F87027a

This Grade II listed building was built about 1824 for Thomas Hall, a West Riding magistrate from Castleford. The stone building was originally called Purston Lodge, but it was renamed Featherstone Hall on the death of the owner. After a succession of owners and tenants, the estate was sold to Featherstone Council in 1930 for £3,600, after which it was used as the Town Hall and a public park. The Hall was sold in June 2003 and suffered a fire on 30 December that year. Plans have been submitted for its conversion into flats.

FEATHERSTONE
Green Lane c1955
F87027b

From Cressey's Corner we look west towards the Featherstone Hotel. Beyond that is the cover of the old aerial flightway, which carried colliery waste onto the muck stacks. The road sign here points towards Leeds, just 12 miles to the north, and within a mile is the old and still rural original village of Featherstone.

FEATHERSTONE, *The New School c1965* F87021

Just off Hardwick Road is Girnhill Infants' School, which opened on 30 April 1960 to accommodate youngsters from the huge housing estate which partly replaced the earlier Coal Board houses seen in the background. Many of these are now boarded up awaiting demolition, marking an end to the area's rich but harsh mining history.

ACKWORTH: A PLACE OF PEACE

ACKWORTH

The Buttercross and the Lychgate c1955 A117009

This pastoral scene is on the Green in High Ackworth. To the left is the church of St Cuthbert, built in 1582 on the site of a Saxon chapel from AD 875. The lychgate, made of Norwegian oak, was built in 1878 in memory of the Rev Kenworthy. The cross dates from the 15th century (it was restored in 2003), while Mr Waller, head gardener at Ackworth Park, built the shelter in the late 1930s. Opposite this view is the Mary Lowther Endowed Hospital for the schoolmaster and six poor men.

ACKWORTH
All Saints' Church c1955 A117003

Overcrowding at St Cuthbert's led to the creation of All Saints' on Moortop at the other end of the village. The church was built in 1888 on land given by the Wheeler sisters from nearby Cleveland Lodge. The east window is dedicated to Julia and Sybilla, who both died before the consecration.

ACKWORTH
The Garage c1955 A117005

Just past the church, beside the nearby roundabout, is the site of the old Cross Roads Garage, now much rebuilt and modernised but still selling cars. Out of picture on the right is the Catholic church of 1939, and behind the trees, left, is a sign for the Beverley Arms.

ACKWORTH, *The Beverley Arms c1955* A117004

Opened in the same year as the Catholic church, this pub and
restaurant remains a popular attraction on this busy interchange.
Car usage has increased over the years, ever since the closure of the
local station on the York to Sheffield line that ran from 1879 to 1951.

HEMSWORTH: BITTER MEMORIES FROM THE KINSLEY EVICTIONS

HEMSWORTH
Market Place 1965 H204020

In forty years the town has seen many changes, like the removal of the old school (centre); the site is now a small garden and seating area. The police station (right) remains, and so do the shops and pubs on that side. The town developed rapidly during the mid 1800s when it became surrounded by coalmines. Many miners came here from the north, and a Scottish accent is still very common hereabouts.

▶ **HEMSWORTH**
Bullenshaw House
c1955 H204023

Before Bullenshaw House
was built, the area was
wooded and provided a
natural playground for
youngsters. During the war
two air-raid shelters were
built into the hill.
Bullenshaw House was a
residential home, but it is
now used as a resource
centre for older people.

◄ **HEMSWORTH**
The Parish Church c1955 H204003

Rebuilt in 1867 by John Loughborough
Pearson, the architect of the eastern
extension of Wakefield Cathedral, the parish
church of St Helen looks down on the town's
market place. On the right is the 1000-year-
old yew tree, which was battered by the great
storm of January 1884, but still survives.
Wakefield Road, centre, leads down to
Kinsley and Fitzwilliam, two former mining
communities. Kinsley was the centre of
conflict in 1905 when a strike led to the
eviction of 100 pit families.

HEMSWORTH, *Vale Head Park c1965* H204029

The building of this peaceful park provided much welcome work for the unemployed after the 1927 recession. Opening in 1932, Vale Head Park was formerly a farmer's field. The spring-fed beck that used to fill the paddling pool behind the trees now flows into the Hemsworth Water Park, opened in 1987 as a leisure facility complete with a sandy beach.

INDEX

NAMES OF SUBSCRIBERS

The following people have kindly supported this book by subscribing to copies before publication.

Mr Fred Banks

Mr Michael H & Mrs Jean Barley of Ossett

John Belcher, in memory of Betty Turner

Mr R & Mrs B Best, & Mrs L Corfield

Mr Frank Blakey

Steve, Elaine & Lisa Blezard from Normanton

Mr & Mrs Peter Brickwood, Outwood

Mr Alan Brickwood, Thornes

Mr & Mrs Melvyn Brickwood, Outwood

Mr S C & Mrs J Brierley, Featherstone

Mr D C & Mrs D W Carr, Ackworth, Yorks

The Carter family, Thornes, Wakefield

Mr Brian Corfield

Morfudd Dixon, Caernarfon

A Dransfield & A Nichol, Featherstone

Mr Christopher J Foster of Wakefield

Mr Haydn J Foster and family, Ossett

Angela J Foster of Huddersfield

Mr J Keith & Mrs Sandra Foster, Wakefield

Rob & Barbara Frost, Adelaide, Australia

Kathleen Y Goddard

Mr B & Mrs B J Greatorex, Pontefract

Bernard Hird, Wakefield

Mr John M & Mrs Jane Hirst of Rothwell

In memory of John Holmes, Wakefield

Thomas George Jordan of Normanton 2004

Mr & Mrs T Kaye, Outwood, Wakefield

To Keith love Barbara 2004

In Memory of (Mum) Olwyn Ramsden Lawton

Mrs S H Lee & Mr G Lee, Pontefract

The Levon Family, Wakefield

Victor & Elsie Limb of Normanton, in memory

Gregor & Helen Lowe, Normanton

Philip Lucas

V J Margrave

Stephen Newton & Lorna Newton

Brian Old

Matthew Page

Neil Phillips, New York, USA

Aaron Robinson & Family

Mrs L Sambrook, Wakefield

Paul Smart

Joan P Smith (nee Worth) of Horbury Bridge

P J Smith

Margart Webster Thornley, Pontefract

In memory of Betty Turner of Castleford

Alan & Deborah Walsh

John & Kathleen Wright

Frith Book Co Titles

www.francisfrith.co.uk

The Frith Book Company publishes over 100 new titles each year. A selection of those currently available is listed below. For latest catalogue please contact Frith Book Co.
Town Books 96 pages, approximately 100 photos. **County and Themed Books** 128 pages, approximately 150 photos (unless specified). All titles hardback with laminated case and jacket, except those indicated pb (paperback)

Amersham, Chesham & Rickmansworth (pb)	1-85937-340-2	£9.99	Devon (pb)	1-85937-297-x	£9.99
Andover (pb)	1-85937-292-9	£9.99	Devon Churches (pb)	1-85937-250-3	£9.99
Aylesbury (pb)	1-85937-227-9	£9.99	Dorchester (pb)	1-85937-307-0	£9.99
Barnstaple (pb)	1-85937-300-3	£9.99	Dorset (pb)	1-85937-269-4	£9.99
Basildon Living Memories (pb)	1-85937-515-4	£9.99	Dorset Coast (pb)	1-85937-299-6	£9.99
Bath (pb)	1-85937-419-0	£9.99	Dorset Living Memories (pb)	1-85937-584-7	£9.99
Bedford (pb)	1-85937-205-8	£9.99	Down the Severn (pb)	1-85937-560-x	£9.99
Bedfordshire Living Memories	1-85937-513-8	£14.99	Down The Thames (pb)	1-85937-278-3	£9.99
Belfast (pb)	1-85937-303-8	£9.99	Down the Trent	1-85937-311-9	£14.99
Berkshire (pb)	1-85937-191-4	£9.99	East Anglia (pb)	1-85937-265-1	£9.99
Berkshire Churches	1-85937-170-1	£17.99	East Grinstead (pb)	1-85937-138-8	£9.99
Berkshire Living Memories	1-85937-332-1	£14.99	East London	1-85937-080-2	£14.99
Black Country	1-85937-497-2	£12.99	East Sussex (pb)	1-85937-606-1	£9.99
Blackpool (pb)	1-85937-393-3	£9.99	Eastbourne (pb)	1-85937-399-2	£9.99
Bognor Regis (pb)	1-85937-431-x	£9.99	Edinburgh (pb)	1-85937-193-0	£8.99
Bournemouth (pb)	1-85937-545-6	£9.99	England In The 1880s	1-85937-331-3	£17.99
Bradford (pb)	1-85937-204-x	£9.99	Essex - Second Selection	1-85937-456-5	£14.99
Bridgend (pb)	1-85937-386-0	£7.99	Essex (pb)	1-85937-270-8	£9.99
Bridgwater (pb)	1-85937-305-4	£9.99	Essex Coast	1-85937-342-9	£14.99
Bridport (pb)	1-85937-327-5	£9.99	Essex Living Memories	1-85937-490-5	£14.99
Brighton (pb)	1-85937-192-2	£8.99	Exeter	1-85937-539-1	£9.99
Bristol (pb)	1-85937-264-3	£9.99	Exmoor (pb)	1-85937-608-8	£9.99
British Life A Century Ago (pb)	1-85937-213-9	£9.99	Falmouth (pb)	1-85937-594-4	£9.99
Buckinghamshire (pb)	1-85937-200-7	£9.99	Folkestone (pb)	1-85937-124-8	£9.99
Camberley (pb)	1-85937-222-8	£9.99	Frome (pb)	1-85937-317-8	£9.99
Cambridge (pb)	1-85937-422-0	£9.99	Glamorgan	1-85937-488-3	£14.99
Cambridgeshire (pb)	1-85937-420-4	£9.99	Glasgow (pb)	1-85937-190-6	£9.99
Cambridgeshire Villages	1-85937-523-5	£14.99	Glastonbury (pb)	1-85937-338-0	£7.99
Canals And Waterways (pb)	1-85937-291-0	£9.99	Gloucester (pb)	1-85937-232-5	£9.99
Canterbury Cathedral (pb)	1-85937-179-5	£9.99	Gloucestershire (pb)	1-85937-561-8	£9.99
Cardiff (pb)	1-85937-093-4	£9.99	Great Yarmouth (pb)	1-85937-426-3	£9.99
Carmarthenshire (pb)	1-85937-604-5	£9.99	Greater Manchester (pb)	1-85937-266-x	£9.99
Chelmsford (pb)	1-85937-310-0	£9.99	Guildford (pb)	1-85937-410-7	£9.99
Cheltenham (pb)	1-85937-095-0	£9.99	Hampshire (pb)	1-85937-279-1	£9.99
Cheshire (pb)	1-85937-271-6	£9.99	Harrogate (pb)	1-85937-423-9	£9.99
Chester (pb)	1-85937-382 8	£9.99	Hastings and Bexhill (pb)	1-85937-131-0	£9.99
Chesterfield (pb)	1-85937-378-x	£9.99	Heart of Lancashire (pb)	1-85937-197-3	£9.99
Chichester (pb)	1-85937-228-7	£9.99	Helston (pb)	1-85937-214-7	£9.99
Churches of East Cornwall (pb)	1-85937-249-x	£9.99	Hereford (pb)	1-85937-175-2	£9.99
Churches of Hampshire (pb)	1-85937-207-4	£9.99	Herefordshire (pb)	1-85937-567-7	£9.99
Cinque Ports & Two Ancient Towns	1-85937-492-1	£14.99	Herefordshire Living Memories	1-85937-514-6	£14.99
Colchester (pb)	1-85937-188-4	£8.99	Hertfordshire (pb)	1-85937-247-3	£9.99
Cornwall (pb)	1-85937-229-5	£9.99	Horsham (pb)	1-85937-432-8	£9.99
Cornwall Living Memories	1-85937-248-1	£14.99	Humberside (pb)	1-85937-605-3	£9.99
Cotswolds (pb)	1-85937-230-9	£9.99	Hythe, Romney Marsh, Ashford (pb)	1-85937-256-2	£9.99
Cotswolds Living Memories	1-85937-255-4	£14.99	Ipswich (pb)	1-85937-424-7	£9.99
County Durham (pb)	1-85937-398-4	£9.99	Isle of Man (pb)	1-85937-268-6	£9.99
Croydon Living Memories (pb)	1-85937-162-0	£9.99	Isle of Wight (pb)	1-85937-429-8	£9.99
Cumbria (pb)	1-85937-621-5	£9.99	Isle of Wight Living Memories	1-85937-304-6	£14.99
Derby (pb)	1-85937-367-4	£9.99	Kent (pb)	1-85937-189-2	£9.99
Derbyshire (pb)	1-85937-196-5	£9.99	Kent Living Memories(pb)	1-85937-401-8	£9.99
Derbyshire Living Memories	1-85937-330-5	£14.99	Kings Lynn (pb)	1-85937-334-8	£9.99

Available from your local bookshop or from the publisher

Lake District (pb)	1-85937-275-9	£9.99
Lancashire Living Memories	1-85937-335-6	£14.99
Lancaster, Morecambe, Heysham (pb)	1-85937-233-3	£9.99
Leeds (pb)	1-85937-202-3	£9.99
Leicester (pb)	1-85937-381-x	£9.99
Leicestershire & Rutland Living Memories	1-85937-500-6	£12.99
Leicestershire (pb)	1-85937-185-x	£9.99
Lighthouses	1-85937-257-0	£9.99
Lincoln (pb)	1-85937-380-1	£9.99
Lincolnshire (pb)	1-85937-433-6	£9.99
Liverpool and Merseyside (pb)	1-85937-234-1	£9.99
London (pb)	1-85937-183-3	£9.99
London Living Memories	1-85937-454-9	£14.99
Ludlow (pb)	1-85937-176-0	£9.99
Luton (pb)	1-85937-235-x	£9.99
Maidenhead (pb)	1-85937-339-9	£9.99
Maidstone (pb)	1-85937-391-7	£9.99
Manchester (pb)	1-85937-198-1	£9.99
Marlborough (pb)	1-85937-336-4	£9.99
Middlesex	1-85937-158-2	£14.99
Monmouthshire	1-85937-532-4	£14.99
New Forest (pb)	1-85937-390-9	£9.99
Newark (pb)	1-85937-366-6	£9.99
Newport, Wales (pb)	1-85937-258-9	£9.99
Newquay (pb)	1-85937-421-2	£9.99
Norfolk (pb)	1-85937-195-7	£9.99
Norfolk Broads	1-85937-486-7	£14.99
Norfolk Living Memories (pb)	1-85937-402-6	£9.99
North Buckinghamshire	1-85937-626-6	£14.99
North Devon Living Memories	1-85937-261-9	£14.99
North Hertfordshire	1-85937-547-2	£14.99
North London (pb)	1-85937-403-4	£9.99
North Somerset	1-85937-302-x	£14.99
North Wales (pb)	1-85937-298-8	£9.99
North Yorkshire (pb)	1-85937-236-8	£9.99
Northamptonshire Living Memories	1-85937-529-4	£14.99
Northamptonshire	1-85937-150-7	£14.99
Northumberland Tyne & Wear (pb)	1-85937-281-3	£9.99
Northumberland	1-85937-522-7	£14.99
Norwich (pb)	1-85937-194-9	£8.99
Nottingham (pb)	1-85937-324-0	£9.99
Nottinghamshire (pb)	1-85937-187-6	£9.99
Oxford (pb)	1-85937-411-5	£9.99
Oxfordshire (pb)	1-85937-430-1	£9.99
Oxfordshire Living Memories	1-85937-525-1	£14.99
Paignton (pb)	1-85937-374-7	£7.99
Peak District (pb)	1-85937-280-5	£9.99
Pembrokeshire	1-85937-262-7	£14.99
Penzance (pb)	1-85937-595-2	£9.99
Peterborough (pb)	1-85937-219-8	£9.99
Picturesque Harbours	1-85937-208-2	£14.99
Piers	1-85937-237-6	£17.99
Plymouth (pb)	1-85937-389-5	£9.99
Poole & Sandbanks (pb)	1-85937-251-1	£9.99
Preston (pb)	1-85937-212-0	£9.99
Reading (pb)	1-85937-238-4	£9.99
Redhill to Reigate (pb)	1-85937-596-0	£9.99
Ringwood (pb)	1-85937-384-1	£7.99
Romford (pb)	1-85937-319-4	£9.99
Royal Tunbridge Wells (pb)	1-85937-504-9	£9.99
Salisbury (pb)	1-85937-239-2	£9.99
Scarborough (pb)	1-85937-379-8	£9.99
Sevenoaks and Tonbridge (pb)	1-85937-392-5	£9.99
Sheffield & South Yorks (pb)	1-85937-267-8	£9.99
Sherborne (pb)	1-85937-301-1	£9.99
Shrewsbury (pb)	1-85937-325-9	£9.99
Shropshire (pb)	1-85937-326-7	£9.99
Shropshire Living Memories	1-85937-643-6	£14.99
Somerset	1-85937-153-1	£14.99
South Devon Coast	1-85937-107-8	£14.99
South Devon Living Memories (pb)	1-85937-609-6	£9.99
South East London (pb)	1-85937-263-5	£9.99
South Somerset	1-85937-318-6	£14.99
South Wales	1-85937-519-7	£14.99
Southampton (pb)	1-85937-427-1	£9.99
Southend (pb)	1-85937-313-5	£9.99
Southport (pb)	1-85937-425-5	£9.99
St Albans (pb)	1-85937-341-0	£9.99
St Ives (pb)	1-85937-415-8	£9.99
Stafford Living Memories (pb)	1-85937-503-0	£9.99
Staffordshire (pb)	1-85937-308-9	£9.99
Stourbridge (pb)	1-85937-530-8	£9.99
Stratford upon Avon (pb)	1-85937-388-7	£9.99
Suffolk (pb)	1-85937-221-x	£9.99
Suffolk Coast (pb)	1-85937-610-x	£9.99
Surrey (pb)	1-85937-240-6	£9.99
Surrey Living Memories	1-85937-328-3	£14.99
Sussex (pb)	1-85937-184-1	£9.99
Sutton (pb)	1-85937-337-2	£9.99
Swansea (pb)	1-85937-167-1	£9.99
Taunton (pb)	1-85937-314-3	£9.99
Tees Valley & Cleveland (pb)	1-85937-623-1	£9.99
Teignmouth (pb)	1-85937-370-4	£7.99
Thanet (pb)	1-85937-116-7	£9.99
Tiverton (pb)	1-85937-178-7	£9.99
Torbay (pb)	1-85937-597-9	£9.99
Truro (pb)	1-85937-598-7	£9.99
Victorian & Edwardian Dorset	1-85937-254-6	£14.99
Victorian & Edwardian Kent (pb)	1-85937-624-X	£9.99
Victorian & Edwardian Maritime Album (pb)	1-85937-622-3	£9.99
Victorian and Edwardian Sussex (pb)	1-85937-625-8	£9.99
Villages of Devon (pb)	1-85937-293-7	£9.99
Villages of Kent (pb)	1-85937-294-5	£9.99
Villages of Sussex (pb)	1-85937-295-3	£9.99
Warrington (pb)	1-85937-507-3	£9.99
Warwick (pb)	1-85937-518-9	£9.99
Warwickshire (pb)	1-85937-203-1	£9.99
Welsh Castles (pb)	1-85937-322-4	£9.99
West Midlands (pb)	1-85937-289-9	£9.99
West Sussex (pb)	1-85937-607-x	£9.99
West Yorkshire (pb)	1-85937-201-5	£9.99
Weston Super Mare (pb)	1-85937-306-2	£9.99
Weymouth (pb)	1-85937-209-0	£9.99
Wiltshire (pb)	1-85937-277-5	£9.99
Wiltshire Churches (pb)	1-85937-171-x	£9.99
Wiltshire Living Memories (pb)	1-85937-396-8	£9.99
Winchester (pb)	1-85937-428-x	£9.99
Windsor (pb)	1-85937-333-x	£9.99
Wokingham & Bracknell (pb)	1-85937-329-1	£9.99
Woodbridge (pb)	1-85937-498-0	£9.99
Worcester (pb)	1-85937-165-5	£9.99
Worcestershire Living Memories	1-85937-489-1	£14.99
Worcestershire	1-85937-152-3	£14.99
York (pb)	1-85937-199-x	£9.99
Yorkshire (pb)	1-85937-186-8	£9.99
Yorkshire Coastal Memories	1-85937-506-5	£14.99
Yorkshire Dales	1-85937-502-2	£14.99
Yorkshire Living Memories (pb)	1-85937-397-6	£9.99

FREE PRINT OF YOUR CHOICE

Mounted Print
Overall size 14 x 11 inches (355 x 280mm)

Choose any Frith photograph in this book.
Simply complete the Voucher opposite and return it with your remittance for £2.25 (to cover postage and handling) and we will print the photograph of your choice in SEPIA (size 11 x 8 inches) and supply it in a cream mount with a burgundy rule line (overall size 14 x 11 inches).
Please note: photographs with a reference number starting with a "Z" are not Frith photographs and cannot be supplied under this offer.
Offer valid for delivery to UK addresses only.

PLUS: Order additional Mounted Prints at HALF PRICE - £7.49 each (normally £14.99)
If you would like to order more Frith prints from this book, possibly as gifts for friends and family, you can buy them at half price (with no additional postage and handling costs).

PLUS: Have your Mounted Prints framed
For an extra £14.95 per print you can have your mounted print(s) framed in an elegant polished wood and gilt moulding, overall size 16 x 13 inches (no additional postage and handling required).

IMPORTANT!

These special prices are only available if you use this form to order . You must use the ORIGINAL VOUCHER on this page (no copies permitted). We can only despatch to one address. This offer cannot be combined with any other offer.

Send completed Voucher form to:
The Francis Frith Collection, Frith's Barn, Teffont, Salisbury, Wiltshire SP3 5QP

CHOOSE A PHOTOGRAPH FROM THIS BOOK

Voucher for **FREE** and Reduced Price *Frith Prints*

Please do not photocopy this voucher. Only the original is valid, so please fill it in, cut it out and return it to us with your order.

Picture ref no	Page no	Qty	Mounted @ £7.49	Framed + £14.95	Total Cost
		1	Free of charge*	£	£
			£7.49	£	£
			£7.49	£	£
			£7.49	£	£
			£7.49	£	£
			£7.49	£	£
Please allow 28 days for delivery			* Post & handling (UK)		£2.25
			Total Order Cost		£

Title of this book . . . .
I enclose a cheque/postal order for £ . . . .
made payable to 'The Francis Frith Collection'

OR please debit my Mastercard / Visa / Switch (Maestro) /Amex card
(credit cards please on all overseas orders), details below

Card Number

Issue No (Switch only)   Valid from (Amex/Switch)

Expires   Signature

Name Mr/Mrs/Ms . . . .
Address . . . .
. . . .
. . . .
. . . . Postcode . . . .
Daytime Tel No . . . .
Email . . . .

Valid to 31/12/07

Free Print - see overleaf

Would you like to find out more about Francis Frith?

We have recently recruited some entertaining speakers who are happy to visit local groups, clubs and societies to give an illustrated talk documenting Frith's travels and photographs. If you are a member of such a group and are interested in hosting a presentation, we would love to hear from you.

Our speakers bring with them a small selection of our local town and county books, together with sample prints. They are happy to take orders. A small proportion of the order value is donated to the group who have hosted the presentation. The talks are therefore an excellent way of fundraising for small groups and societies.

Can you help us with information about any of the Frith photographs in this book?

We are gradually compiling an historical record for each of the photographs in the Frith archive. It is always fascinating to find out the names of the people shown in the pictures, as well as insights into the shops, buildings and other features depicted.

If you recognize anyone in the photographs in this book, or if you have information not already included in the author's caption, do let us know. We would love to hear from you, and will try to publish it in future books or articles.

Our production team

Frith books are produced by a small dedicated team at offices in the converted Grade II listed 18th-century barn at Teffont near Salisbury, illustrated above. Most have worked with the Frith Collection for many years. All have in common one quality: they have a passion for the Frith Collection. The team is constantly expanding, but currently includes:

Paul Baron, Phillip Brennan, Jason Buck, John Buck, Ruth Butler, Heather Crisp, David Davies, Louis du Mont, Isobel Hall, Gareth Harris, Lucy Hart, Julian Hight, Peter Horne, James Kinnear, Karen Kinnear, Tina Leary, Stuart Login, David Marsh, Lesley-Ann Millard, Sue Molloy, Glenda Morgan, Wayne Morgan, Sarah Roberts, Kate Rotondetto, Dean Scource, Eliza Sackett, Terence Sackett, Sandra Sampson, Adrian Sanders, Sandra Sanger, Jan Scrivens, Julia Skinner, David Smith, Miles Smith, Lewis Taylor, Shelley Tolcher, Lorraine Tuck, Amanita Wainwright and Ricky Williams.